Brother Azarias

Culture of the spiritual sense

Brother Azarias

Culture of the spiritual sense

ISBN/EAN: 9783741164897

Manufactured in Europe, USA, Canada, Australia, Japa

Cover: Foto ©Andreas Hilbeck / pixelio.de

Manufactured and distributed by brebook publishing software
(www.brebook.com)

Brother Azarias

Culture of the spiritual sense

CULTURE

OF

THE SPIRITUAL SENSE

BY

Brother AZARIAS

OF THE BROTHERS OF THE CHRISTIAN SCHOOLS
PRESIDENT OF ROCK HILL COLLEGE, MARYLAND

*Signatum est super nos lumen vultus
tui, Domine.*   Ps. IV, 7

NEW YORK
E. STEIGER & CO.
1884

To

HIS MANY FRIENDS

AT HOME AND ABROAD, WHO SO KINDLY THOUGHT OF HIM,

AND STILL MORE KINDLY PRAYED FOR HIM, WHEN SICKNESS

WAS UPON HIM, AND DEATH SEEMED AT HAND,

THIS ADDRESS,

THE FIRST FRUIT OF RECOVERED STRENGTH,

IS AFFECTIONATELY INSCRIBED

BY THE AUTHOR.

PREFACE.

The author delivered the present Address to the Senior students of the College. He now sends it forth to the larger audience outside the College walls. On a former occasion, he undertook to show that much of the erroneous thinking of the day was due to a superficial exercise of the Reason. He therefore laid stress upon its thorough cultivation not simply in its logical faculty, but also in developing the spirit of observation and discrimination of those motives, prejudices, hereditary habits, and undercurrents of thought that contribute so largely towards determining and coloring one's conclusions. He now calls attention to the necessity of recognizing and accepting as a fact the Spiritual and Supernatural Order, and of cultivating the Spiritual Sense. Only in this manner does one include the whole sphere of Knowledge and take the proper point of view from which to note all things in their true relations.

ROCK HILL COLLEGE, November 1, 1883.

CULTURE OF THE SPIRITUAL SENSE.

I.

1. The human soul is the informing principle of the human body; it is one and simple — a monad without quantity or extension — as all spiritual substances are one, simple and unextended; incomplete in itself inasmuch as it must needs be united to the body in order that it may fully exercise all its functions; immaterial, and therefore void of inertness; ever active, ever exercising its activity. According to the mode of its action do we speak of it as having this faculty or that corresponding to the function which it performs. But it is still the same soul, one and undivided, that thinks and feels, that wills and moves and is moved. And when we say that it has certain faculties we simply mean that it exercises certain modes of action by placing itself in certain definite relations with certain objects of thought.* Faculties of the soul are therefore the soul itself viewed in the performance of particular lines of action, and they become more or less developed according to the degree of activity exercised in some one or other

---

* A friend, in reading over the proofsheets, calls my attention to the following passage in St. Thomas, in which the distinction between the soul and its faculties is clearly laid down: Manifestum est quod ipsa essentia animae non est principium immediatum suarum operationum; sed operatur mediantibus principiis accidentalibus. Unde potentiae animae non sunt ipsa essentia animae, sed proprietates ejus. (*De Anima.* XII.) The distinction is important. It is only in God that act and essence are one, for God is most pure actuality. But the soul being one and simple, and therefore void of parts, is the principle of all its activities: whether mediately or immediately, it is outside the scope of this Address to discuss. I am merely laying down, in broadest outline, the soul's operations.

direction. Now it is the soul analyzing, comparing, inferring, co-ordinating, passing from known principles to the discovery of unknown truths ; viewed in this relation, the soul is called Reason, and, under certain aspects, the Illative Sense.* Now it is the soul deciding this to be a good act, and resolving to perform it, or thinking that other to be bad, and avoiding it; so acting, it is called the Moral Sense. Again it is the soul moved to pity by the pathos of a scene painted on the canvas or described in the poem ; as the subject of this emotion it is called the Esthetic Sense. Finally, it is the soul leaving the noise and distraction of the outside world, entering into itself and realizing its own misery and weakness, and seeking the help and strength which it finds not in itself, where they alone are to be found, in the God from Whom it comes and on Whom it depends ; in this highest and noblest action it is called the Spiritual Sense.†

2. The Reason is nourished by intellectual truth ; the Moral Sense is strengthened by the practice of good deeds; the Esthetic Sense is cultivated by the correcting and refining of taste for things beautiful and sublime ; the Spiritual Sense is fostered by the spirit of piety and devotion. This fourfold activity of the soul may be said

---

* "This power of judging about truth and error in concrete matters, I call the Illative Sense" .... "The Illative Sense has its exercise in the starting-points as well as in the final results of thought." Cardinal NEWMAN. *Grammar of Assent.* Chap. IX. This Chapter is an important contribution to the Philosophy of Thought.

† This corresponds rather with the πίστις of Clement of Alexandria, than with the *Sovrintelligenza* of Gioberti. On the use of this latter term in the sense of Gioberti. see an article by the author in the *International Review* for March, 1876, on *The Nature and Synthetic Principle of Philosophy*, pp. 204—206.

to cover the whole of its operations. Over all, and the root and principle of all, giving life and being, aim and direction, weight and measure and intrinsic worth to all, is the soul's own determining power, which we call the Will. In the harmonious development of all four activities is the complete culture of the soul to be effected. The exclusive exercise of any one is detrimental to the rest. The exclusive exercise of the Reason dwarfs the other functions of the soul. It dries up all taste for art and letters and starves out the spirit of piety and devotion. In the constant development of the Esthetic Sense, one may refine the organs of sense and cultivate the sensibility, but if it is done to the exclusion of rigid reasoning and the emotions of the superior soul, it degenerates into sentimentalism and corruption of heart. So also with exclusive Pietism; it narrows the range of thought, fosters the spirit of bigotry and dogmatism, and makes man either an extravagant dreamer or an extreme fanatic. Only when goodness and truth walk hand in hand, and the heart grows apace with the intellect, does the soul develop into strong and healthy action.

3. Again, natural truth is the object of Reason : natural goodness, the object of the Moral Sense ; natural beauty, whether in the physical, moral, or intellectual order, the object of the Esthetic Sense. Herein I include as a natural truth, knowable by the light of Reason, the fact first and supreme above all other facts, that there is a God.* Now, the Spiritual Sense takes in all the truth,

---

* Si quis dixerit, Deum unum et verum, Creatorem et Dominum nostrum per ea, quae facta sunt, naturali rationis humanae lumine certo cognosci non posse; anathema sit. *Constitutio Dogmatica de Fide Catholica.* Can. II. 1.

goodness and beauty both of the natural and revealed orders, and views them in the light of Faith. The same intellectual light still glows, but added thereto is the splendor of God's countenance.* And so the vision of the Spiritual Sense passes from the natural up to the plane of the Supernatural world.

II.

1. Here the Agnostic objects and with the utmost confidence assures us that there is no Supernatural order. He tells you that he has proved Christ a myth, the Gospels clever forgeries and Christianity a huge imposition. He tells you it is all settled beyond controversy; only intellectual babes and sucklings think differently to-day.† And in the name of humanity — he loves humanity exceeding

---

* Signatum est super nos lumen vultus tui, Domine. Ps. IV. 7. Illuminet vultum suum super nos. Ps. LXVI. 2.

† Schrader in the following words, shows how much is involved in this assertion: "Sed quod horribilius est his jam impuris diebus nostris reservatum fuit, quibus 'spurius quidam egressus est vir' contra Dominum Nostrum Jesum Christum castamque sponsam ejus ecclesiam." He is here alluding to Renan. "Infandum scelus, quod consummatum non fuit, nisi negato data opera exclusoque 1. ordine supernaturalium, hinc 2. ordine divino; tum 3. illorum discrimine ab ordine humano; atque 4. tandem ipso everso ordine humanitatis et ejusdem 5. ab ordine brutescentium discrimine negato atque everso. Scilicet negatio copulationis supernaturalis naturalisque ordinis in præsentiarum ad negationem ducit θεανθρώπου: atqui haec negatio attentatio est

I. in totum historicum ordinem, qui nunc pendet a Christo centro:

II. in universum ordinem logicum, qui nunc pendet a Christo perfectæ veritatis doctore:

III. in universum ordinem ethicum, qui nunc pendet a Christo summa morum norma:

IV. in universum ordinem juridicum, qui nunc pendet a Christo Domino supremo legumlatore:

V. et in ipsum tandem ordinem artis, qui jam pendet a Christo divino pulchritudinis exemplari. Videlicet a Christo pendet tota humanitatis dignitas in coelo et in terra!" CLEMENTIS SCHRADER, S. J. De Triplici Ordine Commentarius. pp. 210, 211.

well — and in the name of truth — he reveres truth — he begs you to set aside all such silly notions as that there exists a God, or that His Providence directs the affairs of men, or that you have a soul. This is indeed a new dispensation. It is the gospel of negation, and the Agnostic is its missionary. But in the name of whom or of what does he come? Assuredly, not in the name of common sense, for the common sense of the whole world holds with absolute certainty the very opposite. Not in the name of revelation, for he denies the possibility of a revealed religion. Not in the name of human authority, for he recognizes no authority beyond himself. Not in the name of reason, for in bringing himself to this conviction, he ignores the primary laws of all reason. "It is", says Cardinal Newman, "the highest wisdom to accept truth of whatever kind, wherever it is clearly ascertained to be such, though there be difficulty in adjusting it with other known truth."* Now here is where the Agnostic errs. He has a favorite theory, a pet notion of his own. It is a mere hypothesis that may or may not be true. But he finds difficulty in adjusting it with truths that come home to the highest order of intelligence with an irresistible force. So much the worse for both truth and intellect. His pet conception must stand, and the universally received truths may vanish into oblivion. Of course, his conclusions cannot be broader than his premises. The elements he drops out in the one will naturally be missing in the other. Eliminating the Supernatural order, as a consequence

---

* *Idea of a University. Lecture on Christianity and Scientific Investigation.* p. 462.

there remains in the visible process of his reasoning only the natural order

2. Withal, the Supernatural order exists. It secretly enters into the Agnostic's reasoning and becomes a disturbing element in his calculations. He may ignore it; he may neglect it; he may deny it; but he cannot destroy it. In moral, social and historical discussions, it crops out at the most unexpected moments, or awaits him at the end of his speculations and forces him into monstrous paradoxes.* And strange to say, the Agnostic does not perceive how illogical he is. He even becomes aggressive, and boldly asserts that in recognizing this momentous element in human thought and human action, we thereby lose all claim to science. Now, science, as you are taught, is a methodical treatment of facts according to given principles. By means of what principles and according to what method does the Agnostic arrive at this conclusion? So far as he has a principle at all, it is reducible to this, that what the study of matter does not reveal is a dream, a shadow;† there is no reality beyond the phenomena testified to by consciousness and the senses.‡ That is to say, the Agnostic builds up his materialistic theories upon a principle made expressly to exclude that which he wishes to ignore. Is it just? Is it scientific? And as for method, the Agnostic has none. He holds aloof from all religious thoughts and remains in a state of apathy towards all spiritual issues. He may or may not have a soul; it is unknowable. There may or may not be a God; He also

---

* For instances see Mr. MALLOCK's work, *Is Life Worth Living?* Chap. IX.
† LESLIE STEPHEN. *Dreams and Realities.*
‡ *The Value of Life:* A reply to Mr. Mallock's work. p. 72.

is unknowable. All such questions he regards with sublime indifference. Is this an attitude worthy of a respon-
sible being ?

3. But the Agnostic will reply that he has no other
evidence for the Supernatural than the Supernatural itself,
and that he is asked to believe in this unseen world without
being able to perceive, or weigh, or measure it. True it
is that the evidence of the Supernatural is the Supernatural itself. But it is not true that it may not be per-
ceived and estimated. Has the Agnostic ever seen material
force ? And yet he believes in it and calculates some
of its results as displayed in chemical, electric or other
material manifestations. Even so may the presence of
that mysterious power called Grace be detected. It shapes
the lives of men in a distinct mould. The light of Faith
and the love of God and the peace of heart that dwell in
those living under its influence, leaven their every act and
word and thought, and give their virtues a tone and
character that are lacking in the exercise of the same
virtues by the natural man. Donoso Cortes was one of
the most brilliant intellects of this age. When a young
man he was carried away by the rationalism and superficial philosophy of the eighteenth century, and grew cold
towards the religion of his childhood and his mother.
Proud of his genius, he dreamed only of worldly greatness.
"I was", he writes to his friend Montalembert, "possessed
of a literary fanaticism, a fanaticism for expression, a
fanaticism for beauty of form".* But the death of a
brother whom he loved dearly, and the intimate acquaint-

* *Oeuvres.* Ed. Louis Veuillot. t. I. Int. p. XIV.

ance of a good and virtuous friend in whose example he
discerned the action of grace, caused him to enter into
himself. His eyes were opened. He recognized the
supernatural character of his friend's virtues ⸱ grace began
to work in his own soul, and led him to become an edify-
ing Christian and an uncompromising champion of the
Church. He thus tells the story of his conversion. "Dur-
ing my stay in Paris I lived intimately with M . . . ., and
this man overcame me solely by the life he led. I had
known righteous and good men, or rather I had known
only righteous and good men; still between the rightcous-
ness and goodness of other men and the righteousness and
goodness of my friend, I found an immeasurable distance.
This difference was not one of degree simply; it was one
of kinds of righteousness in all respects distinct. And
upon reflection I clearly saw the difference to be this, *that
the righteousness of others was natural, whereas that of
this man was supernatural or Christian*".* And com-
menting upon his conversion, he adds: "As you see,
neither talent nor reason had any influence in bringing it
about; with my weak talent and my sickly reason, death
might have stricken me down before faith would have come
to me. The mystery of my conversion is a mystery of
tenderness. I did not love God, and God wished me to
love Him; I love Him now, and because I love Him I am
converted".† These are beautiful words revealing the
beautiful simplicity of a great soul. And so, as clearly
as in St. Paul and St. Augustine, may we perceive

---

* *Oeuvres.* Ed. Louis Veuillot. t. II. p. 120.
† *Ibid.* p. 121.

in the good and holy men of our own day, grace abounding.

4. No; the supernatural world is a reality as real as — and in a sense more real than — the natural world. He who denies or ignores it, understands not himself nor humanity nor the universe in which he finds himself. The human heart knows neither rest nor happiness till it becomes sanctified in this mysterious world. Therefore it is, that an Augustine will cry out from the depths of his own experience : "Lord, Thou hast made us for Thyself, and our heart is restless till it reposes in Thee".* And with no less conviction does Spinoza lay it down as a positive truth that the perfect understanding, which with him is equivalent to the life of the intellect — *mentis vita* — is naught else than the apprehension of God and of the attributes and acts which follow from His Divine Nature.† Where, then, is the wisdom of denying a fact so palpable to men standing at such opposite poles of thought as Spinoza and St. Augustine? Those professing such wisdom may indeed be possessed of knowledge varied and practical in things material and of the senses, but concerning things spiritual and of the Supernatural order they live in blind ignorance. It is to be hoped that it is not also wilful ignorance.

III.

1. Let us draw nearer to this mysterious world of grace, and study the secret of that power by which it subdues the fiercest natures and controls the most brilliant

---

* Domine, fecisti nos ad te, et inquietum est cor nostrum donec requiescat in te. *Conf.* Lib. VII.

† *Ethics.* P. IV. App. § IV.

intellects. Not only is the Supernatural a fact, and an
insurmountable one, but it contains in itself the reason
for the existence of the natural; for whilst it supposes
the natural in the order of ideas, in the order of things
it exists prior thereto, and regulates the condition of its
existence. In the Word were all things created. God
spoke and they were. Their ideals dwelt in that eternal
Word. From all eternity, through all time, or rather in a
perpetual Now — for there is neither past nor future in
God* — God contemplates those ideals and the reason
for their existence in the Word. For the Word is the conception of the Divine Intelligence.† It is God conceiving
Himself. And in this Divine Conception the Father
recognizes Himself, and the Son, and the Holy Ghost, and
all other things contained in the Divine Intelligence.
Therefore all knowledge, all wisdom, all created things are
in the Word and exist by reason of the Word.‡

2. And so, St. John, in the sublime hymn with which
he opens his Gospel of love, reveals to us this Word as
co-eternal with the Father, the One by Whom all things
were made, and the source of their life and their light.

---

* Plato expresses this distinction very clearly: "And the terms *it was —*
τὸ τ'ἦν — and *it will be* — τὸ τ'εσται — are generated forms of time, which we
have wrongly and unawares transferred to an eternal essence." *Timaeus.* XIV, 1.

† Dicitur autem proprie Verbum in Deo, secundum quod Verbum signi-
ficat conceptum intellectus. *Summa S. Thomae.* Pars. I. Quaest. XXXIV, Art.
1. Id enim quod intellectus in concipiendo format, est Verbum. Intellectus
autem ipse, secundum quod est per speciem intelligibilem in actu,
consideratur absolute. *Ibid.* ad 2.

‡ Sic ergo uni soli personae in divinis convenit dici, eo modo quo dicitur
.Verbum. Eo verè modo quo dicitur res in verbo intellecta, cuilibet personae
convenit dici Pater enim intelligendo se, et Filium, et Spiritum Sanctum, et
omnia alia quae ejus scientiâ continentur, concipit Verbum: ut sic tota Trinitas
Verbo dicatur, et etiam omnis creatura. *Ibid.* ad 3.

He, the disciple whom Jesus loved, and who was privileged to rest his head upon the bosom of the Incarnate Word, drew therefrom the secret of His Divinity and Personality, and with the directness and simplicity of genius and inspiration, broke through the clouds in which human thought had enveloped that Divine Word, and at once and for ever gave full, clear and distinct expression to that which men hitherto had only stammered :

1. *"In the beginning was the Word, and the Word was with God, and the Word was God.*

2. *The same was in the beginning with God.*

3. *All things were made by Him : and without Him was made nothing that was made.*

4. *In Him was Life and the Life was the light of men."**

Thus it is that in this Divine Person, the Word, we find the cause and the motive for our existence. Here is the source of our life, our intelligence, our very being. The

---

* *St. John.* Chap. 1. The Abbé Baunard, in his life of the Evangelist, thus sums up the philosophic significance of these sublime words, as against the errors that were then rife:

To the Word of the Gnostics, created and born in time, the Evangelist opposes the eternity of the Word: *In the beginning was the Word.*

To the Word of Plato and of the Academy, a superior but purely ideal conception of the human understanding, the Evangelist opposes the reality of the Word and His Divinity: *And the Word was God.*

To the Word of Philo, simple instrument of God in the creative work, the Evangelist opposes the creation by the Word, principle of all that is: *Everything was made by Him.*

To the Dualist system, setting forth two concurring principles of things, the Evangelist opposes the Word, sole principle and sole creator of every contingent being : *All things were made by Him; and without Him was made nothing that was made.*

Finally, to Docetism rejecting the reality of the flesh of Christ, the Evangelist opposed the astonishing formula: *And the Word was made flesh. Life of the Apostle St. John.* Eng. tr. p. 301.

light of our created reason, by which we are enabled to contemplate this great primary truth, is a spark kindled at the focus of the Uncreated Reason.

3. Nor is this all. The creative act, being one of love as well as of power and intelligence, had for its end none other than God Himself. But how raise up the infinitely impotent into participation with the glory of the Infinitely Potent ? – How give such importance to the infinitely small that it may not be lost in the Infinitely Great ? — For how immense so ever the finite may be in itself, when compared with the infinite it becomes as nothing. There is no term of comparison; the ratio of one to the other cannot be expressed.* Divine Love, without obligation or necessity, acting with the full freedom of omnipotence, determined the solution of the mystery. The Word in His Divine Infinitude, touches the finite and takes upon Himself as the most fitting in the whole of Creation† our human nature: *"And the Word was made flesh, and dwelt amongst us"*. By this mysterious act, the chasm between the finite creation and the Infinite Creator became bridged over; human nature was raised up into the sphere of the Supernatural, and all created things were made participators in the glory of the Divinity. Man was rendered worthy of his destiny. He might fall from grace and favor before his heavenly Father, but in the Word made flesh — in the God-Man — he has a propitiator.

---

* This may be made plain by the following algebraic formulæ, in which f = any finite quantity and the symbol ∞ = infinity: $\frac{\infty}{f} = \infty$; $\frac{f}{\infty} = 0$; that is, the ratios between infinity and finiteness run either into infinity or nothing.

† *Summa.* Pars III. Quæst. IV, Art. 2, Jesus Christ assumes human nature in His Divine Person, but not in His Divine Nature. *Ibid.* Quæst. II, Art. 2.

And so, the Word also becomes the Redeemer. In the Word, then, dwell grace and hope and salvation for poor, weak, struggling humanity. It is the fountain, ever flowing, never diminishing, of the love and mercy from which man has drawn grace from the beginning.

> "Tho' truths in manhood darkly join,
> Deep-seated in our mystic frame,
> We yield all blessing to the name
> Of Him that made them current coin".*

4. Here we may rest. We have ascended giddy heights and cannot soar higher. In contemplating the Word we are contemplating that which is the object of God's own complacency. It is the source of all knowledge and the ideal of all perfection. It is the light of the world, the life of nations, the clue to epochs. Its Human Manifestation is the central fact of history, giving meaning and significancy to all other facts. It is the inspiration of whatever is sacred and ennobling in literature. It is the dwelling-place for the ideal in art. It is the guide of conscience, the abode of truth, the light that dispelleth all intellectual and moral darkness and bringeth life and warmth, the vanquisher of evil, and the secret spring of all true joy. The splendor of Its glory shines forth in the beautiful things of nature, and sheds lustre upon the outpourings of grace as revealed in human actions. Loveliness and beauty and grandeur and sublimity in word and work, in color and figure, are, each in its degree, faint glimmerings of the resplendent glory abiding in that Divine Word which is the source and cause of both the natural and Supernatural.

---

* TENNYSON. *In Memoriam*, XXXVI.

IV.

1.   It is the wisdom of true philosophy to take man as
he is and deal with him accordingly.   Now, man is indeed
in his essence and nature a rational animal.   But this de-
finition of the School says not all.   Man is more.   He is
also a child of grace.   No sooner had he been created man
than he became the recipient of God's choicest favors.   And
when, by the Fall, he had forfeited many of his high prerog-
atives, he still retained sufficient grace by which he was
enabled to repent and be converted.   It is within every
man's power to attain the high destiny to which he has
been called; but he can do so only by reason of the saving
grace that flows from the Word.   This is not a law of
to-day or yesterday; it is of all time.   "We are plants",
says Plato, "not of earth, but of heaven; and from the
same source whence the soul first arose, a Divine Nature,
raising aloft our head and root, directs our whole bodily
frame".*   We come from God that we may go back to
Him.   The Word became incarnate for all, merited for all,
died for all, redeemed all in order that all might have life
everlasting.   Ours, and ours alone, will be the fault if we
should wander away from that noble destiny.

> Not in entire forgetfulness,
> Not in utter nakedness,
> *But trailing clouds of glory, do we come,*
> *From God who is our home.*†

2.   Therefore I would have you foster in yourselves
primarily and above all the Spiritual Life.   It is worthy of
your noblest efforts and your most undivided attention.

---

* *Timaeus.* Cap. LXXI.
† WORDSWORTH. *Ode on Immortality.*

No time should be thought too precious to devote to it, for
it deals with the things of eternity; no thought too sustained or too painful, for its object is the Light of all intelligence.   In the prayers that you make to Him who is
the Life and the Light; in the sacraments that are administered to you; in the sermons that you hear and the
doctrinal instructions that are given you, do you imbibe
the food that will nourish and sustain in you the spiritual
life.   And for our souls' sake it is to be hoped that we all
of us receive abundance of this heavenly manna.   This is
the one thing necessary.   But it is not with the Spiritual
Life that I am now concerned; it is rather with the Spiritual Sense.   They are distinct and are not always found
together.   The sentiment of piety and sensible relish for
Divine things may be very weak in a nature that is
spiritually strong.   And also, one may be very weak in the
practice of virtue, and still possess this sentiment to a
high degree of refinement and cultivation.   But I speak of
this Spiritual Sense as a faculty of your soul which requires
culture as does Reason or any other faculty.   And I take
it that should you neglect its cultivation there would be
lacking something to the complete development of your
soul-functions.   Your studies give an outward tendency
to your soul; they withdraw it from itself.   They are
therefore to it a species of distraction.   But the soul has
an inward life; and for the proper development of this
inward life, it behooves it to enter into itself and cultivate
the interior spirit.

3.   This is the function of the Spiritual Sense.   Without
it our thinking were incomplete.   It is an incentive to higher

and superior culture. Would you know why it is that the religious life has been at all times a nursery for learning and a fountain-head of original thought? Much is due to the fact that scholars and thinkers have instinctively sought therein a refuge from the noise and whirl of worldly affairs. But much also is due to the cultivation of the Spiritual Sense. It enlarged their intellectual horizon. It threw upon things an additional and far-reaching light. It gave those men a favorable vantage-ground from which they might survey deeds and doers of deeds with unbiased mind. Sheltered in the sanctuary of religion, away from the storms of political strife and free from the struggles and anxieties, the temptations and distractions that beset their less fortunate brothers' battling through the turmoil of life, their souls rested in a peaceful calm beneath this spiritual sky that brought joy and contentment to their hearts, and shed upon them a light which beamed forth from their countenances, even as it enhanced the clearness of their intellectual vision. And so, when they looked out upon the world and the things of the world, they saw more distinctly the needs and wants and short-comings of humanity, and were the first to apply the remedy. They led the van in arts and letters, in science and education, and in all that goes to make up a people's civilization. With no slight reason, then, does Renan speak of monastic institutions as a great school of originality for the human mind.*

4. We have nothing to fear from Religion. She is our strength and our support. "The splendor of the Divine truths received into the mind, helps the understanding; and

---

* Mais il est certain qu'en perdant les institutions de la vie monastique l'esprit humain a perdu une grande école d' originalité. *Etudes d'Histoire Religieuse.* p. 318.

far from detracting from its dignity, rather adds to its nobility, keenness and stability." So speaks His Holiness, Leo XIII, in his noble vindication of Christian philosophy.* Such is also the experience of Maine de Biran whom Cousin pronounces the greatest metaphysician that has honored France since Mallebranche.† And his testimony is all the more valuable because it is the outcome of long and circuitous wanderings through the mazes of philosophic errors, with here und there a glimpse of light, till finally in his mature years, after much groping and great toil, the full splendor of truth burst upon him. He says: *"Religion alone solves the problems put by philosophy.* She alone tells us where to find truth, absolute reality. Moreover, she shows us that we live in a perpetual illusion when we estimate things by the testimony of the senses, or according to our passions, or even according to an artificial and conventional reason. *It is in raising ourselves up to God and seeking union with Him by His grace, that we see and appreciate things as they are.* Certain it is that the point of view of the senses and passions is not at all that of human reason; still less is it that of the superior reason, which, strengthened by religion, soars far above all earthly things."‡ These are not the words of a cloistered monk, nor of a religious teacher. He who penned them had been a materialist in philosophy and a worldling in practical life, and though he had outgrown his materialism, and cast off much of the spirit of the world,

---

* Encyclical *Æterni Patris*, 1879.

† *Nouvelles Considérations sur le Rapport du Physique et du Moral.* Ouvrage Posthume de Maine de Biran, Préface de M. Cousin, p. VI.

‡ *Journal Intime.* Quoted in A. NICOLAS: *Etude sur Maine de Biran.* (Paris, 1858.) This monograph is a philosophical gem, which deserves to be better known.

still at the time he penned them, he did not acknowledge himself a Christian. They are his inmost convictions wrung from him in self-communion by the spirit of truth.

V.

1. But I need not go beyond yourselves for further reason why you should cultivate the Spiritual Sense. You now look out upon the world decked in all the roseate hues that your young imaginations weave; your fancies filled with schemes of ambition; bent upon achieving success in some one or other walk of life, you are eager, even to impatience, to enter upon your course; and you may think it a loss of time, a diverting you from your main purpose, to enter seriously upon the cultivation of this Spiritual Sense. On the contrary, you will find in it a help. The present is only a passing phase of your existence. Youth soon fades and strength decays; and as shock after shock in your struggle through life, demolishes one after another the air-castles which you so long and so laboriously constructed, you will more and more feel the necessity of ceasing to lean upon broken reeds and of looking within your soul's interior for an abiding comfort. And if you find there but emptiness, even as you have found hollowness and deceit without, you will grow hardened and cynical. But if, on the other hand, you have learned to commune with yourself and to make your soul's interior the guest-chamber in which to entertain the Divine Word — the Emmanuel dwelling within you — in Him you will find renewed strength to fight your battles with the world, to help you in trouble, to soothe you in pain, and to console you in sorrow and affliction. And so, in cultivating

the Spiritual Sense you are also educating yourselves up to the larger views of life, and learning the great lesson of patience and forbearance.

2. And there is another moment — a supreme moment — when the language of the soul, the sentiment of piety and relish for Divine things, the habit of sweet communion with your Savior, will be to you a blessing and a comfort. It is when you are prostrate on the pallet of sickness, and life is ebbing fast, and the helpless body seems to be sinking down abysmal depths with the weight of its own inertness. From time to time the soul's flickering flame lights up into a sudden blaze of consciousness and animation, as if wrestling hard to be free. Dear friends and near relatives may be there, hovering around you, ministering to your every want and gratifying your least desire. But in the questioning look with which they watch the face of your physician, and the anxious glances that they cast upon you, and the subdued whisperings in which they speak their worst fears, you learn that you are beyond all human aid. Fainter flickers the vital spark and weaker grows the frame, and loving faces look upon you with a more wistful look, and loving forms pass before you with a more stealthy tread; but they are to you as though they were not. Fainter and feebler you become, and the world recedes farther and farther from you, and those you love so dearly seem afar off, and the distance between you and them grows more and more. You feel yourself sinking into unconsciousness, and you know that your next waking will be in another world, beyond the reach of everything in life around which your heart-strings are twined. The last rites

of the Church are administered to you, and as your senses
are about shutting out forever the sights and sounds of this
world, you catch as the faint echo of a far-off voice, the
words of the priest, "Go forth, O Christian soul". Happy
will you be in that dread hour, if, when you appear before
the Divine Searcher of hearts, the pure light of the Word
penetrates no corner that you did not already know, and
reveals no sin that has not already been repented of and
atoned for. Thrice happy will you be when you meet the
Divine Presence face to face, if, having cultivated the
Spiritual Sense and acquired a relish for Divine truths, you
find that you are familiar with the language of love and
adoration, of praise and thanksgiving, which should be
yours for all eternity, and that you are not as a stranger in
a strange land, but rather as a child welcomed home to his
Father's House after a life-long exile. Wise indeed were it
that we all of us learn in time this language which must be
ours throughout eternity.

VI.

1. There are two manuals of instruction and initiation
into this mystical language of the soul, which I would especially recommend to you. The one is the Book of the Gospels.
You know its contents; but you must never weary of its pe-
rusal. You will always find in it something new. It treats
of a subject that never grows old. We cannot hear enough
of Him, the Meek One, walking among men and doing good
wherever he went. Open the Book reverently and lovingly,
and let the light of His Blessed Face shine out upon you from
its inspired pages. Sweetly and simply it traces His footsteps;
in loving accents it recounts the words He spoke, the deeds

He did, the miracles He wrought. It reveals the God-Man. It tells of His sufferings from the manger in Bethlehem to the cross on Calvary. It tells of His patience and forbearance, of His humility and modesty, of His compassion for sinners and His hatred for hypocrisy. His words are as balm to the bruised, rest to the weary, peace to the restless, joy to the sorrowing, and light to those groping in the dark. They penetrate all hearts because they flow from a heart loving man with an infinite love. Our familiarity with them from our childhood up may lead us to lose sight of their infinite worth. The sublimest hymn that was ever poured forth from the lips of man in prayer and the praise of his Creator is the *Our Father*. In its grandeur it rises from the lowest depths of man's nothingness to the throne of Infinite Majesty; in its pathos it searches the heart, touches its feebleness and exposes its wants, with the simplicity and tenderness of a child leaning upon a fond and merciful father. It is at once supplication, exhortation, instruction, praise and worship. Again, the Sermon on the Mount embodies all that there is of good and perfect in moral thought, moral word, and moral work in the whole life of humanity. And so I might go on enumerating the beauties and sublimities of this marvelous Book and never tire, never get done. Its beauty is untold; its wisdom is unfathomable. They are the beauty and the wisdom of Him who is the ideal of all loveliness and the source of all wisdom.

2. That other book which I would recommend to you has garnered a few of the lessons revealed in these Gospels and bound them together in rich and ripe sheaves of thought. A rare harvesting indeed is this book. It is known in every

tongue and its praises have been sung in every note. Next
to its original and source it is the most popular book ever
written. I speak of *The Imitation of Christ*, which Fon-
tenelle without exaggeration well styles the most beautiful
book that ever came from the hands of man.* It has been
admired by all classes of thinkers and all shades of creeds.
The staunch Tory, Doctor Johnson, loved it and used to
speak of it as a good book to receive which the world opened
its arms.† The infidel Jean Jacques Rousseau wept over it.‡
John Wesley published an edition of it as food for the hungering souls to whom he ministered in the Durham coal-pits
and on the Devonshire moors. Bossuet called it a book full
of unction; St. Charles Borromeo, the world's consoler; and
Sir Thomas More said that the book, if read, would secure
the nation's happiness. Surely, a book receiving praise from
so many and such diverse sources is worthy of your intimate
acquaintance, and it will be to me a great pleasure to intro-
duce to you both the author and the book. The author was
Thomas Hämerken of Kempen, commonly known as Thomas
à Kempis (1380–1471). We will first consider the man and
his times; afterwards, we will discuss the spirit, the philosophy and the influence of the book.

VII.

1. The century in which Thomas Hämerken saw the
light, was the transition period between the Mediæval and
the Modern world. The Crusades had done their work;
the Gothic Cathedral had been built; the Miracle-Play had

---

* Le plus beau livre qui soit parti de la main d'un homme, puisque l'Evan-
gile n'en vient pas.
† BOSWELL's *Johnson*, Vol. II. p. 143.
‡ *Dublin University Magazine*, June 1869.

ceased to instruct; Thomas of Aquin had put the finishing hand to Scholastic Philosophy and left it a scientific monument worthy of his genius and the age; Dante had crystallized the faith and science, the fierce hate and the strong love, the poetry, the politics and the theology, the whole spirit of Mediævalism in his sublime allegory. And now that old order was breaking up, and in the awakening of the new much anarchy prevailed. In the general crumbling away of institutions, the human intellect seemed bewildered. A groping and a restlessness existed throughout; there was a yearning of men after they knew not what, for the night was upon them and they were impatient for the coming of the dawn. Where were they to seek the light? The ignorant and the obstinate, without either the requisite knowledge or the necessary patience to discover the laws of nature, sought to wrest from her the secrets of which she is possessed, by the process of magic, astrology and simulated intercourse with spirits.* Hecate was their inspiring genius.

2. The learned sought the light, on the one hand, through the mists and mazes of the old issue of Nominalism and Realism, which had been revived by William of Ockham (d. 1347), and continued by John Buridan (d. after 1350), Albert of Saxony (who taught at Paris about 1350—60), Marsilius of Inghen (d. 1392), and the zealous Peter of Ailly (1350—1425).† In their gropings they gathered up little more than an abundance of error, aridity and intellectual pride. Others, following in the wake of Petrarch and Bocca-

---

* See GÖRRES. *La Mystique*, trad. par. M. Ste-Foi. Partie III. *La Mystique Diabolique*. t. IV. Chap. VIII, XIV.

† UEBERWEG. *History of Philosophy*. Eng. tr. Vol. I. p. 465.

cio, began to cultivate an exaggerated taste for the ancient
classics and to revive the spirit of Paganism. Children
were instructed in Greek,* and the pedantic quarrels of
grammarians divided cities and even whole provinces.†
Others again, weary of the barren disputations of the
Schools, sought the light in union with the Godhead through
the dark and unsafe paths of Mysticism. Master Eckhart
proclaimed it their goal and only refuge. He undertook to
point out the way, but became lost in the mazes of Neo-
platonism and Pantheism. Under his influence, whole
nations, impelled by an indefinite yearning for spiritual
life, rose up as one man, in universal clamor for mystical
union with the Godhead. They became intoxicated with
the New Science. He had taught them that the creation
of the world and the generation of the Word were one act;
that the soul pre-existed in God from all, eternity; that the
Light of the Word was inseparable from the light of the
soul, and that in union with that Word were to be found
perfection and knowledge.‡

3. Although Eckhart tried to hedge in these dangerous
tenets with various safe-guards and fine-spun distinctions.

---

* Ambroise, de l'ordre des Camaldules, au commencement de 1400,
trouvait dans Mantoue des enfants et des jeunes filles versés dans le grec. CANTU.
Histoire Universelle. t. XII, p. 578.

† Les querelles des pédants hargneux intéressaient, divisaient les villes et
les provinces. Ibid. p. 589.

‡ "The Light, which is the Son of God, and the shining — das Ausscheinen
— of that light in the creature-world are inseparable. The Birth of the Son and
the Creation of the world are one act." STÖCKL. Geschichte der Philosophie. § III,
6, p. 494. Also 10, p. 495. "The soul, like all things, pre-existed in God . . .
Immanent in the Divine Essence, I created the world and myself." UEBERWEG.
History of Philosophy. Vol. I. § 106, in which Eckhart's teaching is accounted
for at length by Dr. Adolf Lasson. The article in Stöckl is far more satisfactory.

the people, in their ignorance and enthusiasm, broke loose from all restraint and fell into deplorable disorders. Large numbers formed themselves into societies having as spiritual directors laymen who claimed to be initiated into the secrets of this mystical union with the Godhead. This was a condition of things anomalous at it was dangerous. Sometimes, indeed, under this lay direction, the people made real spiritual progress, as did the society known as the Friends of God under the guidance of that mysterious layman who so successfully led the celebrated Tauler into the way of this mystical life.* More frequently, they went beyond all control and became mere fanatics, as the Beguines and Begards.† Tauler (1300 — 1361) took the yearning multitude by the hand and led them in the path which he had trodden. So powerful was his eloquence and so great the influence that he wielded, that even at this day his name is a magic wand capable of stirring the hearts of the descendants of the thousands along' the Rhine, who clung upon his lips and eagerly fed their hungering souls with the words of life that fell from them. And whilst the rugged earnestness of Tauler pierced their hearts, the gentle suavity of Henry Suso (1300—1365), the Minnesinger of the love of God, swayed them with no less force and helped to dissipate the atmosphere of false mysticism and erroneous doctrines in which they were enveloped.

---

* See *Life of Tauler*, prefixed to his Sermons, edited and translated into French by M. Ch. Ste-Foi. (Paris 1855). Vol. I, p. 7 et seq.

† When the organization was dissolved by Pope John XXII, it numbered more than three hundred thousand in Germany alone. GöRRES. *La Mystique*. t. I. p. 131. They were so called from their institutor, Lambert Begha, who established the organization in 1170.

VIII.

1. To this extent had Mysticism become a passion, when Gerhard Groote established the Brothers of the Common Life. The mystical spirit entered into their rule of living, but in so new and practical a form that they become known as Brothers of the New Devotion. It pervades the books they wrote; its spirit was in the very atmosphere of their schools. The children attending them became imbued with it. Amongst those children was Thomas à Kempis. He afterwards became a member of the Order, was ordained priest, and lived to the advanced age of 91 years. We read nothing eventful in his life. Like the Venerable Beda, from his youth up he had borne the sweet yoke of religion. Like Beda also, it had been a pleasure for him to read and teach and write and transcribe what he found best in sacred and profane literature. And that the intellect might not grow barren in the mechanical exercise of transcribing the thoughts of others, it was made a rule that the Brothers should cull, each for himself and according to his taste, some of the beautiful sayings and maxims of the Fathers and saints, and add thereto pious reflections.* This was a labor of love for Thomas, and in performing it he was sowing and fertilizing the seeds of that special book that was to be the child of his genius.

2. Another source of inspiration for that book was the beautiful example of his Brothers. His convent was a spiritual garden in which were tended with great care all the virtues of the religious life. He need only remember and record. Not only in his great work, but in the numerous

---

* These collections were cal ed *Rapiaria*.

lives of the Brothers that he has left us, he never tires of expressing his appreciation of their devotion, regularity and spirit of faith. And they were equally edified by his amiable character and great humility. They held him in honor and esteem, and his influence amongst them was great.* Ono of the Brethren remembers as an event in his life, how he had seen. him and spoken with him: "The Brother who wrote *The Imitation* is called Thomas . . . . This writer was living in 1454, and I, Brother Herman, having been sent to the general chapter in that year, spoke to him."† Nor was he less appreciated outside his convent walls. The Cistercian monk Adrien de But, stops the chronicle of political events to say how he edified by his writings, especially his master-piece, which the good monk not inappropriately styles "a metrical volume."‡ And so, his fame has continued to grow broader, ripple after ripple, till it fills the whole world. And yet, he shrank from notoriety; he loved retirement; he dreaded gossip.§ On, on, through the years of his long life, through

---

* Among the small and peaceful circle of the religious Mystics, no man exercised so important an influence as Thomas Hämerken of Kempen. Gieseler. *Compend. Eccl. History.* V. p. 73.

† Mgr. J. B. Malou. *Recherches sur le véritable auteur de l'Imitation.* p. 82.

‡ Hoc anno frater Thomas de Kempis, de Monte Sanctae Agnetis professor ordinis regularium canonicorum, multos, scriptis suis divulgatis, aedificat; hic vitam Sanctae Lidwigis descripsit *et quoddam volumen metrice super illud: qui sequitur me. Chroniques relatives a l'histoire de la Belgique*, publiées par M. le Baron Kervyn de Lettenhove. t. I. *The Imitation*, as written by'à Kempis is both metrical and rhythmical. This is the conclusion of Dr. Hirsche after long and careful study of the original MS. Henry Sommalius, in 1599, first divided each chapter into paragraphs, and in the 17th century several editors sub-divided the paragraphs into versicles.

§ "Valde devotus, libenter solus, et nunquam otiosus." *MS.* 11,841, Bibl. de Borgogne, Brussels, printed for the first time in Appendix to *Recherches sur le véritable auteur de l'Imitation*, par Mgr. J. B. Malou, 2me Ed. p. 388.

the vigor of youth, through the maturity of manhood, through the gathering shadows of old age, he plied his pen and scattered broadcast devout books. Let us approach still nearer.

3. Figure to yourselves a man of less than medium height,[*] rather stout in body, with forehead broad, and a strong Flemish cast of features, massive and thoughtful, bespeaking a man of meditative habits; his cheeks tinged slightly brown; his large and lustrous eyes looking with a grave and far-off look, as though gazing into the world of spiritual life in which his soul dwelt. This is Thomas à Kempis as he appeared to his contemporaries. Still another glimpse of him as he walks and speaks with his Brothers, has been sketched with a loving hand: "This good Father, when he was walking abroad with some of the Brotherhood, or with some of his other friends, and suddenly felt an inspiration come upon him — namely, when the Bridegroom was willing to communicate with the bride, that is, when Jesus Christ his Beloved, did call to his soul as His elect and beloved spouse — was wont to say, 'My beloved brethren, I must now needs leave you', and so, meekly begging to be excused, he would leave them, saying, 'Indeed it behooves me to go; there is One expecting me in my cell.' And so they accordingly granted his request, took well his excuse and were much edified thereby."[†] In this reverential manner was his memory cherished. We are not surprised to learn that a great many, being attracted by his reputation for science and sanc-

---

[*] "Hic fuit brevis staturae, sed magnus in virtutibus." *Ibid.*

[†] *Opera Omnia Th. de Kempis.* Ed. Georg Pirckhamer. Nuremberg 1494. fol. XXXV. KETTLEWELL. *Thomas à Kempis and the Brethren of the Common Life.* Vol. I. p. 33. Mgr. MALOU. *Recherches,* p. 84.

tity, flocked around him, to cultivate his acquaintance and
to pursue their studies under his guidance.*

4. What was the inner life of this attractive soul?
What were the trials, the struggles with self, the temptations
through which he passed? — Surely, he who is both philosopher and poet of the interior life in all its phases, must have
traversed the rugged path leading up to perfection with an
observant eye for all the dangerous turns and treacherous
pitfalls that lurk on the way. Above all, he must have loved
much. "The passion", says Michelet, "which we meet in this
work, is grand as the object which it seeks; grand as the
world which it forsakes." And in this love he found strength
to overcome every obstacle. In another work he thus lays
bare his soul: "Sometimes my passions assailed me as a
whirlwind; but God sent forth his arrows and dissipated
them. The attack was often renewed, but God was still my
support."† And in his great book he occasionally gives us a
glimpse of himself. Thus we see him at the beginning of his
religious career in doubt and great mental anxiety as to
whether or no he will persevere. "He presently heard within
him an answer from God, which said, 'If thou didst know
it, what wouldst thou do? Do now, what thou wouldst do
then, and thou shall be secure.' And being herewith comfort-
ed and strengthened, he committed himself wholly to the will
of God, and his anxious wavering ceased."‡ In another place§

---

* HARDENBERG. *MS. Life of Wessel*, a disciple of Thomas à Kempis. Quoted
by ULLMAN. *Reformatoren vor der Reformation*. 2. Bd. S. 738. Eng. tr. Vol. II.
p. 271.

† *Soliloquy of the Soul.* See Chaps: XV, XVI, XVII.

‡ Bk. I. Chap. XXV, 2.

§ Bk. III. Chap. XXIX.

we find him sending up cries for strength and resignation, such as could only come from a heart bleeding and lacerated with wounds inflicted by calumny and humiliation.* But it is only a soul that rose above the spites and jealousies of life that could speak the words of comfort and consolation therein to be found. "Verily", hath it been beautifully said, "only a breast burning with pity — a breast that hath never wounded another breast — could have offered that incense to heaven, that dew to earth, which we call *The Imitation*."† Such was the author. He had learned to repress every inordinate desire or emotion, until in his old age he was content with solitude and a book. "I have sought rest everywhere", was he wont to say, "but I have found it nowhere except in a little corner with a little book."‡

IX.

1. It is interesting to study the literary structure of *The Imitation*, and note the traces of authorship running through it. We will glance at it for a moment. First of all and above all, the book is saturated through and through with the Sacred Scriptures. You can scarcely read a sentence that does not recall some passage now in the Old, now in the New Testament. It reflects their pure rays like an unbroken mirror. To transcribe the Bible had been a labor of love for the author. A complete copy of it in his own neat handwriting is still extant. Echoes of beautiful passages from the spiritual writers that went before him reverberate through the pages of this book which is none

---

* Charles Butler. Life prefixed to Bishop Challoner's translation of *The Imitation*. p. VII.

† William Maccoll in *Contemporary Review*, Sept. 1866.

‡ Charles Butler. *loc. cit.* p. VIII.

the less original. The author drew from St. Gregory the Great.* St. Bernard seems to have been a special favorite.† So was St. Francis of Assisi.‡ He drew from St. Thomas.§ He drew from St. Bonaventura.** He even drew from the Roman Missal.†† He also lays the pagan classics under contribution. He quotes Aristotle.‡‡ He quotes Ovid.§§ He quotes Seneca.*** And there are some remarkable coincidences in expression between himself and Dante.††† He even quotes the popular sayings of his day.‡‡‡ In a word, as with the poet, whatever love inspired, no matter the speech in which the voice came, he wrote at her dictation.§§§

2. In both language and spirit the book exhales the atmosphere of Mysticism in which it was conceived and written. Its very terms are the terms of Mysticism. And

---

* Cf. Gregory, *Cura Pastoralis*, and *Imitation*, Bk. IV. Chap. V.

† Cf. the Hymn *Jesu, dulcis memoria*, and Bk. II. Chaps. VII, VIII.

‡ Cf. *Epist.* XL, and Bk. III. Chap. L–8.

§ Cf. Office for Corpus Christi, and Bk. IV. Chap. II, 1; also Chap. XIII, 2, 17.

** Cf. the Hymn *Recordare Sanctae Crucis* and Bk. II. Chap. XII, 2. The Toulouse Sermons attributed to St. Bonaventura, having so many extracts from *The Imitation* are no longer regarded as authentic. See Mgr. MALOU. *Recherches sur le véritable auteur de l'Imitation*, pp. 198—202.

†† Cf. Prayer for XVth Sunday after Pentecost, and *Im.* Bk. III. C. LV, 6; Post. Com. IV Sunday in Advent, and Bk. IV, Chap. IV.

‡‡ Aristotle. *Metaphysics.* I, 1, in Bk. I. Chap. II, 1.

§§ Ovid. Lib. XIII. *de Remed. Am.* In Bk. I. Chap. XIII, 5.

*** Seneca. *Ep.* VII, in Bk. I. Chap. XX, 2.

††† Cf. Dante. *Inferno.* Canto III and Canto VI, with Bk. I. Chap. XXIV.

‡‡‡ Bk. II. Chap. IX, 1.   The expression is:
　　　　　　　Satis suaviter equitat,
　　　　　　　Quem gratia Dei portat.

§§§　　　Io mi son un che quando
　　　Amore spira, noto, e in quel modo
　　　Ch'ei detta dentro, vo' significando. — DANTE —

if we would understand the book thoroughly we must make tangible to ourselves this mystical state. In the human soul, there is and has been at all times a strong and irrepressible yearning after the higher spiritual things of the unseen Universe. It is not given to all to attain its dizziest heights. It may not even be well for all to aim thereat. But it is something to be proud of, to know that our humanity has reached that state in its elect few. And what is the mystical state? — It is a striving of the soul after union with the Divinity. It is therefore a turning away from sin and all that could lead to sin, and a raising up of the soul above all created things, "transcending every ascent of every holy height, and leaving behind all Divine lights and sounds and heavenly discoursings, and passing into that Darkness where He is who is above all things".* In this state the soul is passively conscious that she lives and breathes in the Godhead, and asks neither to speak nor think. Her whole happiness is to be. She has found absolute Goodness, absolute Truth, and absolute Beauty; she knows it and feels it and rests content in the knowledge. She seeks nothing beyond. She has left far behind her all practical and speculative habits. Her faculties are hushed in holy awe at the nearness of the Divine Presence.† Memory has ceased to minister to her; Fancy and Imagination walk at a distance and in silence, fearing to obtrude themselves upon the Unimagined Infinite; Reason is prostrate and abashed before the Incomprehen-

---

* Dionysius Areopagita. *De Mystica Theologiâ*. Cap. I, § 3. t. I. Col. 999. *Patrol. Graecae*. Ed. Migne. t. III.

† See Tauler. *Sermon* for the Sunday after Epiphany; trad. Ste-Foi. t. I. p. 130.

sible; Understanding remains lulled in adoration before the
Unknowable. She is overshadowed by the intense splendor of the Divine Glory, and filled -- thrilled through and
through -- with the dread Presence, she is raised above
the plane of our common human feelings and sympathies
into the highest sphere of thought and love and adoration
attainable in this life, and is thus given a foretaste of
Heaven. In this state the soul apprehends with clearness
mysteries that are entirely beyond her ordinary power of
conception. Such was the experience of a Francis of
Assisi, a Henry Suso, a Tauler, a Loyola, a Teresa of
Jesus. But this experience became theirs only after they
had passed through much tribulation of spirit, and their
souls had been purified; for it is only to the clean of heart
that it is given to become intimately united with God in
this manner. Men of proud thought and vain desire, have
attempted without this purification to attain that state;
but invariably they became lost in illusions, were confound-
ed, and fell into the deepest follies. Therefore it is that this
union is safely sought only through the Redeemer. And so we
find the books attributed to the Areopagite make the Chalice
of the Redeemer the central point of all Christian mysteries;
the Chalice being according to them the symbol of Providence which penetrates and preserves all things.* And
this symbol passes down the ages, gathering around it feats
of chivalry and love and bravery — adventure and prowess
which are also symbolic — and men speak of it as the Holy
Grail, which only such as the suffering Tituriel and the

---

* Crater igitur cum sit rotundus et apertus, symbolum est generalis pro-
videntiae quae principio fineque caret atque omnia continet penetratque. Dion.
Areop. *Ep.* IX. *Tito Episcopo.* § III. *Patrol. Graecae.* Ed. Migne. t. III. Col. 1110.

pure Galahad are permitted to behold.* What is it all but a beautiful allegory typifying the struggles of the devout soul before it is permitted to commune with God in this mystical union?

X.

1. Thomas à Kempis knows no other way by which to lead the Christian soul to the heights of perfection and union with the Divinity than the rugged road trodden by Jesus. The opening words of *The Imitation* strike the key-note with no uncertain tone: *"He that followeth Me walketh not in darkness",† saith the Lord. These are the words of Christ, by which we are taught to imitate His life and manners, if we would be truly enlightened and be delivered from all blindness of heart . . . . . Whosoever would fully and feelingly understand the words of Christ, must endeavor to conform his life wholly to the life of Christ."‡* In this manner does the author give us purely and simply, without gloss or comment, the spirituality of the Gospel. He does not flatter human nature. He merely points out the narrow and rugged road to Calvary. The "royal way of the holy Cross" is the only safe way: *"Go where thou wilt, seek whatsoever thou wilt, thou shalt not find a higher way above, nor a safer way below, than the way of the holy Cross".§* And here the pious author, in descanting on the merits of the Cross, becomes truly poetical: *"In the Cross is salvation; in the Cross is life; in*

---

* The symbol of the Chalice is older than Christianity. It was adopted from the Dionysian mysteries of the Greeks and given a Christian meaning. See GÖRRES. *La Mystique.* t. I. p. 78.

† John VIII, 12.

‡ *Imitation.* Bk. I. Chap. t. 1, 2.

§ Bk. II. Chap. XII.

*the Cross is protection against our enemies; in the Cross is
infusion of heavenly sweetness; in the Cross is strength
of mind; in the Cross is joy of spirit; in the Cross is the
height of virtue; in the Cross is the perfection of sanctity.
There is no salvation of the soul, no hope of everlasting
life, but in the Cross. Take up therefore thy Cross and
follow Jesus and thou shall go into life everlasting."** Thus
it is that in the language of à Kempis the Cross symbolizes
all Christian virtue; and bearing one's trials and troubles
with patience and resignation is walking on the royal road
of the Cross. It supersedes the symbol of the Chalice.

2. For the student, *The Imitation* is laden with beautiful lessons. The pious author must have had his own
scholars in his mind's eye in penning many a passage. He
never tires of recalling to them that there is something
better than vain words and dry disputations. *"Surely
great words do not make a man holy and just.....†
Many words do not satisfy the soul.....‡ Meddle not
with things too high for thee; but read such things as may
rather yield compunction to thy heart, than occupation to
thy head."§* He distinguishes between the reading that
goes home to the heart, and that which is merely a matter
of occupation. The distinction is an important one. It
defines the functions of the Spiritual Sense. One to whom
I have already introduced you, draws the same line. I
give you his words. Notice how closely the philosopher
and man of the world, writing four centuries after, coin-

* *Ibid.*
† Bk. I. Chap. I, 3.
‡ *Ibid.* Chap. II, 2.
§ *Ibid.* Chap. XX, 1.

cides with the monk. "I am", says Maine de Biran, "as
agitated by my books and my own ideas, as when occupied
with worldly matters or launched in the vortex of Parisian
life . . . I fancy that I am going to discover my moral and
intellectual welfare, rest and internal satisfaction of mind,
the truth I seek, in every book that I scan and consult;
as though these things were not within me, down in the
very depths of my being, where with sustained and pene-
trating glance, I should look for them, instead of gliding
rapidly over what others have thought, or even what I myself have thought . . . . My conscience reproaches me with
not having thoroughly sounded the depths of life, with not
having cultivated its most earnest parts, and with being too
occupied with those amusements that enable one to pass
imperceptibly from time to eternity".* In good truth,
men may go through life, discoursing upon the things of
life, formulating their views of the diverse subjects that
call for definite opinion; and yet, for want of this introspec-
tion, this self-communion, this thoughtfulness of God's
presence within them, they may indeed possess many and
varied accomplishments, but these are all of the outward
man. The inner man is starved to a skeleton. This is
why all great thinkers, all the founders of religious orders
as well as of schools of philosophy, Pythagoras and Socrates
as well as Benedict and Loyola, have laid stress upon the
culture of this interior spirit. It is not merely the opinion
of a pious author; it is the doctrine of the Gospel. made the
wisdom of humanity.

---

* *Journal Intime.* Apud Nicolas. Etude sur Maine de Biran, p. 54.

3. Again, the author lays down the conditions under which study may be pursued with advantage. He shows the greater responsibility attached to human knowledge, and counsels the students to be humble. *"The more thou knowest, and the better thou understandest, the more strictly shalt thou be judged, unless thy life be also the more holy. Be not therefore elated in thine own mind because of any art or science, but rather let the knowledge given thee make thee afraid. If thou thinkest that thou understandest and knowest much; yet know that there be many more things which thou knowest not".* Bear in mind that the author is not simply inculcating the modesty and diffidence that belong to every well-educated person, and that may accompany great intellectual pride. He goes deeper, and insists upon true humility.† *"If thou wilt know and learn anything profitably, desire to be unknown and little esteemed. This is the highest and most profitable lesson : truly to know and despise ourselves".‡*

4. The pious author is no less earnest in counseling the student to be simple and pure. *"By two wings a man is lifted up from things earthly, namely, by Simplicity and Purity. Simplicity ought to be in our intention; Purity in our affections. Simplicity doth tend towards God; Purity doth apprehend and taste him . . . . . If thy heart were sincere and upright, then would every creature be unto thee a living mirror, and a book of holy doctrine. There*

---

* Bk. I. Chap. II, 3.

† Cardinal Newman, in one of his most beautiful Discourses, shows how modesty accompanied by pride has taken the place of the Christian virtue of humility in the modern world. *Idea of a University.* Discourse VIII, §9, pp. 254—258.

‡ Bk. I. Chap. II, 3, 4.

is no creature so small and abject, that it representeth not the goodness of God. If thou wert inwardly good and pure, then wouldst thou be able to see and understand all things well without impediment. A pure heart penetrateth heaven and hell."* Doctrine as beautiful as it is true. Only to the clean of heart is it given to see God in heaven. Only to the clean of heart is it also given to recognize the splendor of His glory in the beautiful things that He has created. The poetry and chivalry of the Middle Ages vie with each other in extolling this pearl among the virtues. Percival's purity of heart wins for him the rare privilege of beholding the Holy Grail. Launcelot fails in his quest because of his sin. Sir Galahad's virgin heart makes him tenfold strong against his foes :

> "My good blade carves the casques of men,
> My tough lance thrusteth sure,
> My strength is as the strength of ten
> *Because my heart is pure*".†

XI.

1. The philosophy of *The Imitation* may be summed up in two words. It is a philosophy of Light and a philosophy of Life : the Light of Truth and the Life of Grace. Both the one and the other, à Kempis seeks in their source and fountain-head. He does not separate them. It is only in the union of both that man attains his philosophic ideal. Vain words and dry speculations, scholastic wrangling and religious controversy, may furnish food for man's vanity, but they are unable to nourish his soul. And so, the devout au-

---

* Bk. II. Chap. IV, 2, 3.
† TENNYSON. *Sir Galahad.*

thor, with Clement of Alexandria, with Augustine and Aquinas, ascends to the Incarnate Word—the Divine Logos—as the source whence proceeds all truth both natural and revealed, for the criterion and the ideal of human knowledge. Here he finds unity and harmony. And if human opinions oppose one another, those alone can be true which are compatible with the revealed and certain dogmas of the Church.* Therefore, he begs the student to hush the clash of systems, and seek above and beyond all system and all caviling the truth pure and simple as it emanates from the Godhead. In his day the clashing of scholastic opinion was loud and fierce, and the din of the Schools so filled the air that he steps aside from his usual course of ignoring the issues and contests of the outside world and asks: "What matters it to us about genera and species?" Upon the solution of this problem hinged the endless disputations between Nominalism and Realism ever since Roscelin revived the issue nearly four centuries previously. The students adopted one or other according to their nationality. In the University of Prague the Bohemian students were Realists, whilst those of Germany were Nominalists. And when a crisis occurs in the affairs of that institution, we see 24,000 of the German Nominalists abandon its halls and establish a new University in Leipsig.†

---

* Human reason is feeble and may be deceived, but true faith cannot be deceived. All reason and natural search ought to follow faith, not to go before it, nor to break in upon it. Bk. IV. Chap. XVIII, 4, 5.

† Cantu. *Hist. Univ.* t. XII, p. 293. Some say 40,000. See Lenfant. *Hist. de la Guerre des Hussites.* Utrecht. 1731. pp. 59, 60, and *Histoire du Concile de Constance.* t. I, p. 30, 31. Of course, the immediate cause of the difficulty was the retrenchment of certain privileges of the German professors and students by Wenceslaus at the instigation of John Huss.

2.   Thomas à Kempis has in his book no place for these strifes.   In a philosophic poem, which is only less sublime than that with which St. John opens his Gospel, because it is an echo thereof, the devout author lays down the doctrine of truth that runs through his book, even as it has been the actuating principle of his life: *"Happy is he whom Truth by itself doth teach, not by figures and words that pass away, but as it is in itself.   Our own opinion and our own sense do often deceive us, and they discern but little.   What availeth it to cavil and dispute much about dark and hidden things, for ignorance of which we shall not be reproved at the day of judgment?   It is a great folly to neglect the things that are profitable and necessary, and to choose to dwell upon that which is curious and hurtful.   We have eyes and see not. And what have we to do with genera and species ?   He to whom the Eternal Word speaketh is delivered from many an opinion.   From one Word are all things, and all things utter one Word; and this is the Beginning which also speaketh unto us.* No man without that Word understandeth or judgeth rightly.   He to whom all things are one, he who reduceth all things to one, and seeth all things in one; may enjoy a quiet mind, and remain at peace in God.   O God, who art Truth itself, make me one with Thee in everlasting love. It wearieth me often to read and hear many things: in Thee is all that I would have and can desire. Let all teachers hold their peace; let all creatures be silent in Thy light; speak Thou alone unto me."†* Can you imagine a sublimer passage coming from a human hand?

---

* Principium, qui et loquor vobis.   St. John. VIII, 25.

† Bk. I. Chap. III.

3. This is not a system of philosophy. Like Pascal and St. Augustine, à Kempis soars above system, and in the mystical language so well known and understood in his day, he reduces all philosophy to this principle of seeing things in the light emanating from the Word. *"From one Word are all things, and all things utter one Word . . . No man without that Word understandeth or judgeth rightly."* In vain would you search heaven or earth for a more elevating, more correct, or more fruitful principle in philosophy. Was the author Realist? Was he Nominalist? He was neither. Not that he was not interested in philosophic discussions; for did he not take a keen interest in them, he never would have penned those sublime pages. But his genius sought greater freedom than it could have found in any system. No sooner is one committed to a school, than one has to pare down, or exaggerate, or suppress altogether truths and facts to tally with the system taught by the school. Neither truth nor fact are the outcome of system or school; prior to either, both truth and fact existed. Systems and schools in confessing themselves such, acknowledge by the very fact that they do not deal with truth whole and entire as truth, but with certain aspects of truth seen from a given point of view. They may be good, they may even be necessary, as aids in acquiring truth; but they are not to be identified with it. They are, so to speak, the scaffoldings by which the edifice of truth may be constructed, and as such are to be laid aside as soon as the structure is completed. In this spirit was it that Thomas à Kempis thought and worked.

4. Was the author opposed to learning? The many expressions in which he speaks so lightly of purely human

knowledge or scholastic disputations, would lead one to think that he was inclined to disparage all such. Nothing was farther from his intention. His whole life was devoted to the work of education. He had formed and sent forth, well equipped, many distinguished pupils and disciples.* He never lost his taste for books. To transcribe and spread abroad good books both in sacred and profane learning had been his delight. In one of his sermons he exclaims, "Blessed are the hands of such transcribers! Which of the writings of our ancestors would now be remembered, if there had been no pious hands to transcribe them?"† But as *The Imitation* treats of the finite and the temporal in their relations with the infinite and the eternal, naturally all things purely human, though not in themselves insignificant, suffer by comparison. In this sense does he define his position: "*Learning, science — scientia — is not to be blamed, nor the mere knowledge of anything whatsoever, for that is good in itself and ordained of God; but*", he adds, looking at things from his elevated point of view, and in all truth may he say it, "*a good conscience and a virtuous life are always to be preferred before it.*" Not the knowledge he condemns, but the pride, the vanity, the worldliness that are sometimes found in its

---

* Ullman says: "He encouraged susceptible youths to the zealous prosecution of their studies, and even to the acquisition of a classical education. Several of the most meritorious restorers of ancient literature went forth from his quiet cell, and he lived to see in his old age his scholars, Rudolph Lange, Count Maurice of Spiegelberg, Louis Dringenberg, Antony Liber, and above all, Rudolph Agricola and Alexander Hegius laboring with success for the revival of the sciences in Germany and the Netherlands. Accordingly Thomas was not without scientific culture himself or the power of inspiring a taste for it in others." *Reformatoren vor der Reformation.* Bd. II. loc. cit. Eng. tr. Vol. II, p. 135.

† Sermon on the text: *Christus scribit in terra.*

train. "*Because many endeavor rather to get knowledge than to live well, they are often deceived, and reap either none or but little fruit.*" In like manner, the author places true greatness, not in great intellectual attainments, but rather in great love and humility: "*He is truly great that hath great love. He is truly great that is little in himself and that maketh no account of any height of honor.*"*

XII.

1. Here we find ourselves at the second word in which the philosophy of *The Imitation* is summed up. It is not only the Light of Truth; it is also the Life of Grace. This life consists in the practice of the Christian virtues; the practice of the Christian virtues leads up to union with Christ; and union with Christ is consummated in the Holy Eucharist. Such is the author's philosophy of life, and in its development does his genius especially glow. He is mystical, eloquent, sublime. He soars into the highest regions of truth in which meet both poetry and philosophy. Following in the footsteps of Christ, heeding His words, living in intimate union with Him, loving Him with a love that counts no sacrifice too great, trampling under foot all things displeasing to Him, bearing one's burden cheerfully for His sake — such is the life of the soul as revealed in this wonderful book. And the author lays stress on the all-important truth that this life should primarily be built upon doctrine. Conscience must be instructed and trained to form correct decisions : "*My words are spirit and life, and not to be weighed by the understanding of man. . . . .*

---

* Bk. I. Chap. III.

*Write thou My words in thy heart, and meditate diligently
on them, for in time of temptation they will be very needful
for thee"* . . . . .* Then Love steps in and fructifies the
soul and makes it bear good actions, actions acceptable
and pleasing to God. It is the vital principle energizing
the world of Grace. And here the author bursts forth into
a canticle of love that finds in every soul a responsive
chord: *"Love is a great thing, yea, a great and thorough
good . . . . . Nothing is sweeter than Love, nothing more
courageous, nothing higher, nothing wider, nothing more
pleasant, nothing fuller nor better in heaven and earth;
because Love is born of God, and can rest but in God above
all created things."* — But you must read the whole poem to
understand and taste its great worth.† And then, note
how this canticle of love is followed by a more practical
commentary, in the form of a dialogue between Christ and
the soul, all written with the most consummate art.:

"CHRIST. *My son thou art not yet a courageous and
wise lover.*

SOUL. *Wherefore sayest Thou this, O Lord?*

CHRIST. *Because for a slight opposition thou givest
over thy undertakings, and too eagerly seekest consolation.
A courageous lover standeth firm in temptation, and giveth
no credit to the crafty persuasions of the enemy. As I
please him in prosperity, so in adversity am I not unpleas-
ing to him. A wise lover regards not so much the gift of
him who loves him, as the love of the giver."*‡

---

* Bk. III. Chap. III, 1, 4. — *Ibid.* Chap. IV, 3.

† Bk. III. Chap. V.

‡ *Ibid.* Chap. VI.

2. Forthwith, the loving soul is instructed in the diverse ways of guarding and preserving grace and virtue, of overcoming temptations, of fleeing and contemning the world, of trying to be meek and lowly and forbearing, and of seeking intimate union with the Beloved. The inclinations of nature, the windings and subterfuges of passion, the dangers from within oneself and the troubles and annoyances that come from without, are all treated with a terseness, clearness, simplicity and unction that are not met with outside of the Sacred Scriptures from which they are reflected. But the devout soul is especially to seek strength and comfort and consolation in union with Christ in the Sacrament of the Holy Eucharist. It contains food for the hungering, healing for the sick; it is the fountain at which the weary and parched soul may slake her thirst; it is the fruition of life, the goal of all struggle, the crowning of all effort. Hear how beautifully the pious author expresses the soul's great need for this saving food: *"Whilst I am detained in the prison of this body, I acknowledge myself to stand in need of two things, to wit, food and light. Unto me, then, thus weak and helpless Thou hast given Thy Sacred Body for the nourishment both of my soul and body; and Thy Word Thou hast set as a light unto my feet. Without these two I should not be able to live, for the word of God is the light of my soul, and Thy Sacrament the bread of life..... Thanks be unto Thee, O Thou Creator and Redeemer of mankind, who to manifest Thy love to the whole world, hast prepared a great supper, wherein Thou hast set before us to be eaten, not the typical lamb, but Thy most Sacred Body and Blood,*

*rejoicing all the faithful with this holy banquet, and re-
plenishing them to the full with the cup of salvation in
which are all the delights of paradise; and the holy angels
do feast with us, but yet with a more happy sweetness.*"*

3. Thus it is that heaven and earth center in this
Sacrament. All the yearnings of the devout soul for union
with the Godhead find their consummation in the worthy
reception of our Lord in this Sacrament of His love. Every
act of virtue is an act of preparation for its reception in the
future and of thanksgiving for past Communions. And so
the Holy Eucharist becomes the central object of all spiritual life. All this is developed with great ingenuity in the
Fourth Book of *The Imitation*. There are several editions
with this Book omitted. Those making the omission, little
think that they are losing sight of the principle and the
motives underlying the other books. But so it is. They
are constructing an arch without a key-stone. They are
giving us the play of Hamlet with the parts of Hamlet
omitted. They are indeed still distributing good and
wholesome thoughts; but at the same time they are de-
stroying the unity of the book and mistaking its philosophy.
It is no longer Thomas à Kempis; it is Thomas à Kempis
diluted and seasoned to suit individual palates.

4. A recent writer equally mistaken as to the importance of the Fourth Book as a clue to the others, imputed to
the pious author motives which he would have repudiated,
and assigned his book a purpose for which it was never in-
tended. "Its quick celebrity", this writer tells us, "is a
proof how profoundly ecclesiastical influence had been

---

* Bk. IV. Chap. XI, 4, 5.

affected, for its essential intention was to enable the pious to cultivate their devotional feelings without the intervention of the clergy . . . . . The celebrity of this book was rather dependent on a profound distrust everywhere felt in the clergy both as regards morals and intellect".* The assertion is gratuitous. There was nothing in the life or character of the author to warrant the statement. It is contradicted by the work itself. No man speaks more reverently of the functions of the Altar, or holds in greater esteem the dignity of the priesthood than does this same Thomas à Kempis, himself a worthy priest. *"Great is the dignity of priests, to whom that is given which is not granted to angels; for priests alone rightly ordained in the Church, have power to celebrate and consecrate the Body of Christ . . ."†* And he thus concludes his beautiful eulogy on the priest at the altar: *"When a priest celebrates, he honors God, he rejoices the angels, he edifies the Church, he helps the living, he obtains rest for the dead, and makes himself partaker of all good things."‡* Thus it is that Thomas places the priest between God and the people as their mediator through the sacrifice of the Mass. Surely he could establish no stronger bond of union between clergy and laity. Where, then, is the distrust of which this writer speaks? You may search the book from cover to cover and you will seek in vain for a single word tending by any

---

* DRAPER. *Intellectual Development of Europe.* p. 470. Mr. Lecky calls this work "extremely remarkable." *History of European Morals.* Vol. I. p. 105. The writer has found it remarkable in its systematic efforts at misreading history and misinterpreting events.

† Bk. IV. Chap. V, 5.

‡ *Ibid.* 6.

manner of means, directly or indirectly, to promote or widen the estrangement of the clergy from the laity. Another writer, a Protestant, regarded Thomas à Kempis in this same relation, but his conclusion was the very reverse. He read, as every truth-loving historian must read, that the pious author "recognizes the existing hierarchy and ecclesiastical constitution in their whole extent, together with the priesthood in its function of mediating between God and man, and . . . . . on every occasion insists upon ecclesiastical obedience as one of the greatest virtues".* This is the whole spirit and intention of à Kempis. And the secret of the celebrity of *The Imitation* goes deeper than the popularity of the hour. Let us consider it for a moment.

XIII.

1. How, it may be asked, was the author able to compass within the covers of this slender volume, so much wisdom, such a vast spiritual experience, such beautiful poetry and profound philosophy. And he has done all this with a grasp and terseness of expression to which no translation has ever been able to do justice. It is because Thomas à Kempis is more than a pious monk, picking up the experiences of the Saints and Fathers who preceded him; he is one of the world-authors; and *The Imitation* is so clearly stamped with the impress of his genius, that wherever men can read they recognize it as a book that comes home to their business and bosoms for all time. Go where you will, you will perceive its silent influence working for good, and upon natures that seem least prepared to be affected by it. Thus we read how a Moorish prince shows a missionary visiting him, a

---

* ULLMANN. *Reform. vor der Ref.* loc. cit. Eng. tr. Vol. II. p. 156.

Turkish version of the book, and tells him that he prizes it above all others in his possession.* That prince may not have been a good Mohammedan in so prizing this little book;† but if he read it with sincerity and thoughtfulness he was all the better man for it. The transition from the cold and fixed fatalism, the barren piety and fierce tribe-spirit of the Korân to the life and warmth and soothing words of *The Imitation*, must indeed have been to him a new revelation that helped to burst the bands and cerements of many a Mohammedan prejudice.

2. Again, the book has always been a consoler in tribu-lation. Louis XVI, when a prisoner, found great comfort in its pages, and read them day and night. La Harpe, in his love and admiration for what in his day was considered elegant literature, thought the book beneath his notice, even as the Humanists before him had regarded St. Paul. But La Harpe comes to grief, and imprisoned in the Luxembourg, meets with it, and, opening it at random, reads: "*Ecce adsum! ecce ego ad te venio quia invocasti me. Lacrymae tuae, et desiderium animae tuae, humiliatio tua et contritio cordis inclinaverunt me et adduxerunt ad te.*"‡ These touching words seemed to come directly out of the mouth of the Con-soler Himself. It was like an apparition. He says: "I fell on my face and wept freely." Ever after *The Imitation* was one of La Harpe's most cherished books.

---

* Avertissement d'une ancienne traduction publiée en 1663, prefixed to the edition of Abbé Jauffret. p. X.

† A book hath been sent down unto thee: and therefore let there be no doubt in thy breast concerning it . . . Follow that which hath been sent down unto thee from thy Lord; and follow no guide besides him. *Korân.* Chap. VII, 1.

‡ Lib. III. Cap. XXI, 6.

3. Once more. A woman of superior genius grandly weaves into one of her most powerful novels the great influence which this book wields for good. The heroine is represented with her young soul stifling in the atmosphere of sordid aim and routine existence, her desires unsatisfied, her yearnings finding no outlet; groping in thickest darkness, impulsive, thoughtless, imprudent, and withal well-meaning. Trouble and misfortune have come upon her, and she has not yet learned the lesson of Christian patience and long-suffering. Her restive soul beats against the cage of circumstances with hopeless flutter. An accident puts her in possession of a copy of *The Imitation*. She reads the book. It thrills her with awe, "as if she had been wakened in the night by a strain of solemn music telling of beings whose soul had been astir while hers was in stupor." It is to her the revelation of a new world of thought and spirituality. She realizes that life, even in her confined sphere of action and routine existence, may be ennobled and made worth living. Was this woman transcribing a chapter from her own life? In reading these magnificent pages, we feel that what George Eliot so graphically recorded of Maggie Tulliver, she had found engraven on the heart of Marian Evans.* This is all the more remarkable, as she did not recognize the Divine source of inspiration whence à Kempis drew so copiously. But she too had her soul-hungerings, and found many a pressing question answered by "this voice out of the far-off Middle Ages", much more efficiently than in feeding on the husks of Positivism and Agnosticism. And with her experience of

---

* George Eliot is the *nom de plume* of Marian Evans, successively Mrs. George Lewes and Mrs. Cross.

the magic book well might she pay it this eloquent tribute: "I suppose that is the reason why the small, old-fashioned book, for which you need only pay sixpence at a book-stall, works miracles to this day, turning bitter waters into sweet-ness, while expensive sermons and treatises, newly issued, leave all things as they were before. It was written down by a hand that waited for the heart's promptings; it is the chronicle of a solitary, hidden anguish, struggle, trust, and triumph, not written on velvet cushions to teach endurance to those who are treading with bleeding feet on the stones. And so it remains to all time a lasting record of human needs and human consolations; the voice of a brother who, ages ago, felt, and suffered, and renounced, in the cloister, per-haps, with serge and gown and tonsured head, with much chanting and long fasts, and with a fashion of speech different from ours, but under the same silent far-off heavens, and with the same passionate desires, the same strivings, the same failures, the same weariness."* Not with the same failures, for this good monk sought only God and God was with him; not with the same weariness, for possessing God in his heart, he was filled with joy and in all gladness of soul he took up his burden and bore it cheerfully.

XIV.

1. Here is the secret of the magic influence wielded by *The Imitation.* Pick it up when or where we may, open it at any page we will, we always find something to suit our frame of mind. The author's genius has such complete control of the subject, and handles it with so firm a grasp,

---

* *The Mill on the Floss.* Bk. IV. Chap. III. p. 272.

that in every sentence we find condensed the experience of ages. It is humanity finding in this simple man an adequate mouth-piece for the utterance of its spiritual wants and soul-yearnings. And his expression is so full and adequate because he regarded things in the white light of God's truth, and saw their nature and their worth clearly and distinctly, as divested of the hues and tints flung around them by passion and illusion. He probed the human heart to its lowest depths and its inmost folds; he searched intentions and motives and found self lurking in the purest; he explored the windings of human folly and human misery and discovered them to proceed from self-love and self-gratification. But this author does not simply lay bare the sores and wounds of poor bleeding human nature. He also prescribes the remedy. And none need go away unhelped. For the foot-sore who are weary with treading the sharp stones and piercing thorns on the highways and by-ways of life; for the heart aching with pain and disappointment and crushed with a weight of tribulations; for the intellect parched with thirsting after the fountain of true knowledge; for the soul living in aridity and dryness of spirit; for the sinner immersed in the mire of sin and iniquity, and the saint, earnestly toiling up the hill of perfection — for all he prescribes a balm that heals, and to all does he show the road that leads to the Life and the Light. And for this reason have I attempted to give you a glimpse of the treasures contained in his little book, that you may through it in a special manner cultivate the Spiritual Sense.

Sublime truths these, which we have been contemplating. If I knew a nobler or a more elevated doctrine, you should have it. As it is, I have placed before you the highest philosophic ideal, that the most fruitful in thought and word and work. You may not grasp its full meaning, or my expression of it may have been inadequate to its sublime conception; be this as it may, I still present it to you with the conviction that it is best for you. I have no heart for the mere negations of criticism or the barrenness of controversy. They may be good in their way; they are good and necessary in their way, for they help to remove error and prejudice. But they bear within themselves none of the germs of life. And thought is starving and the soul is becoming chilled for want of the warmth of life and the nourishment of life-giving food in men's teachings. Great intellects, hungering and thirsting, grope in the cold and the dark for spiritual meat and drink with an earnestness and a yearning that are rarely witnessed in the history of thought. Back of the Rationalism and Agnosticism of the day, may we read a strong religious feeling crying out for life and light and warmth. Could those intellects ascend the heights traversed by the great geniuses in whose company we have been — could they see things as Plato occasionally saw them, as with still keener vision St. John saw them, and as Clement and Augustine and Aquinas and à Kempis saw them, — they too would find that rest and that fulness of life, that belong to those dwelling in the broad day-light of God's truth.

II.
THE DEVELOPMENT OF ENGLISH LITERATURE: THE OLD ENGLISH PERIOD.

New York: D. APPLETON & Co.   Cloth.   Price $1.25

It must be said that Brother Azarias has written an able and interesting text-book in his professional line. Especially in regard to the earliest times of Christianity in England, and to the relation between the Teutonic immigrants and the old inhabitants of Great Britain and Ireland, does our author show his best paces. In some respects he has written a text-book superior to any we know of as now in use. What he knows he knows thoroughly, so thoroughly; indeed, that he can afford to treat Old English questions with the imaginativeness necessary to the best, most interesting kind of writing. * * * * * * There are few writers so well prepared in what might be termed the technique of Old English history and literature. * * * His chapter on the Kelt and Teuton is admirable.   *(New York Times.)*

The style of the book is graphic, yet there is frequently an abruptness by which grace is sacrificed. The Brother's treatment of mental characteristics and natural surroundings as sources of the peculiar quality of English literature is careful and correct, and he shows plainly how the different conquests of England and her harsh climate have influenced the literary productions of the olden time. *(Boston Daily Advertiser.)*

III.
PSYCHOLOGICAL ASPECTS OF EDUCATION.

New York: E. STEIGER & Co.   Paper.   Price $0.10

A brief pamphlet of not many pages; but terse, elegant, full of vigor and clear analysis, like everything that comes from the pen of the gifted President of Rock Hill College. *(American Catholic Quarterly Review.)*

We have seldom come across a more thorough and well-digested essay on the above intricate subject than a paper read before the University Convocation of the State of New York, at Albany, July 11. 1877. * * * The whole paper is remarkable for wide acquaintance with the great problem of education, and it brings out its psychological aspects with a keen and clear delineation and closeness of observation which give permanent value to the essay.   *(New York Star.)*

IV.
ON THINKING.

New York: E. STEIGER & Co.   Large Paper.   Price $0.20

It is original, striking, and, I consider, adapted to make readers think. * * * Religion must be making progress among you, under God's blessing, when it has such intelligent and large-minded exponents.
(John H. Cardinal Newman.)

This is a profoundly thoughtful essay, and reveals a highly philosophic mind in the author. He touches off admirably the cant and shallowness of the present day, which comes of too much reading and too little thought.   *(Chicago Pilot.)*

STEIGER'S French Series.

AHN'S French Primer. By Dr. P. HENN. Boards $0.25. (Great care has been bestowed upon the typographical execution of this little book, the perplexing difficulty of the *silent* letters being alleviated by the use of distinguishing outline and hairline type.

AHN'S French Reading Charts. 20 Plates with Hand-book for Teachers. By Dr. P. HENN. $1.00. (These Wall Charts are printed in very large type, the *silent* letters being shown by outline type cut expressly for the purpose.)

The same. The 20 Plates mounted on 10 Boards. $3.75 net. Mounted on 10 boards and varnished. $5.00 net.

(AHN'S French Primer and French Reading Charts may be advantageously used as an introductory course to *any French Grammar*.)

AHN'S Practical and Easy Method of Learning the French Language. By Dr. P. HENN. First Course. (Comprising a fundamental Treatise on French Pronunciation, French and English Exercises, Paradigms, and Vocabularies.) Boards $0.40.

*Key to same. Boards $0.25 net.

AHN'S Practical and Easy Method of Learning the French Language. By Dr. P. HENN. Second Course. (Comprising a Series of French and English Exercises, Conversations, Elements of French Grammar with Index, and full Vocabularies. Boards $0.60.

*Key to same. Boards $0.25 net.

AHN'S Practical and Easy Method of Learning the French Language. By Dr. P. HENN. First and Second Courses, bound together. Half Roan $1.00.

AHN'S Elements of French Grammar. By Dr. P. HENN. Being the Second Part of AHN-HENN'S Practical and Easy Method of Learning the French Language. —Second Course— printed separately. Boards $0.35

AHN'S First French Reader. With Foot-notes and Vocabulary. By Dr. P. HENN. Boards $0.60; Half Roan $0.80.

AHN'S First French Reader. With Notes and Vocabulary. By Dr. P. HENN. Boards $0.60; Half Roan $0.80.

These two editions of one and the same book differ solely in the typographical arrangement of Text and Notes. In the latter the Notes are given separately on the pages following the 75 pieces of Text; in the former each page has at its bottom exactly so much of the Notes as is needed to explain the French Text above. In respect to Vocabulary, etc., both editions are alike.

*Key to AHN'S First French Reader. By Dr. P. HENN. Boards $0.30 net.

AHN'S Second French Reader. With Foot-notes and Vocabulary. By Dr. P. HENN. Boards $0.80; Half Roan $1.00.

AHN'S Second French Reader. With Notes and Vocabulary. By Dr. P. HENN. Boards $0.80; Half Roan $1.00.

*Key to AHN'S Second French Reader. By Dr. P. HENN. Bds $0.40 net

AHN'S French Dialogues. Dramatic Selections with Notes. Number One. (Specially suitable for young ladies.) Boards $0.30; Cloth $0.40.

AHN'S French Dialogues. Dramatic Selections with Notes. Number Two. (Specially suitable for young gentlemen.) Boards $0.25; Cloth $0.35.

AHN'S French Dialogues. Dramatic Selections with Notes. Number Three. (Specially suitable for young ladies.) Boards $0.30; Cloth $0.40.

Additional volumes of this Series of *French Dialogues*, which fully meet the requirements of advanced students are in press, and will shortly be published.

AHN'S Manual of French Conversation. In press.

AHN'S French Letter-writer. In press.

Collegiate Course.

C. A. SCHLEGEL. A French Grammar. For beginners. Half Roan $1.50.

C. A. SCHLEGEL. A Classical French Reader. With Notes and Vocabulary. Half Roan $1.20.

[* These *Keys* will be supplied to teachers only upon their direct application to the publishers.]

The AHN-HENN Latin Text-Books
☞ superior to others. ☜

At St. Mary's College, North East, Pa., where **Latin** is being studied very **thoroughly in a six years' course**, the results attained by the use of the *AHN-HENN First* and *Second Latin Books* have been so very satisfactory that the President and Professors desired the existing volumes of the *AHN-HENN Latin Course* to be further extended so as to meet all the requirements of **full college study**, and for this purpose *AHN-HENN'S Complete Latin Syntax* and its companion volume, the *Manual of Latin Prose Composition* have been issued. With these two new volumes the *AHN-HENN* **Latin Course** is suitable for **college study** no less than its other volumes — the *Method*, the *Manual*, and the *Short Latin Course* — are **unexcelled** for **Preparatory Classes** of Colleges, for **Schools, Academies** and **private study.**

For the same College the *AHN-HENN German Method* and the *AHN-HENN French Method* have also been selected as the text-books to be used hereafter exclusively.

We are glad to refer to this instance of the adoption of the *AHN-HENN German* and *French Courses* in consequence of the excellence of the several volumes of the **Latin Series;** heretofore we have in numberless cases seen that the Latin, and the French or German had been adopted in consequence of the satisfaction which one or the other of the latter two Courses had given in the course of years. Everywhere teachers were glad to displace old, cumbersome, difficult and unsatisfactory Methods by the *AHN-HENN* books, which make **study easy** while they teach **all that** is really **necessary to learn,** without wasting any of the pupils' time on matters of no value—and actually worse than useless.

We beg to refer to the following extract from a letter:

COLLEGE OF THE CHRISTIAN BROTHERS.

St. Louis, Mo., Sept. 6th, 1883.

We have examined the sample copies of the AHN-HENN Latin Course which you so kindly mailed to us, and have decided to use it exclusively in our Institution.

We do not hesitate to say that it surpasses any "Course" published in this country. — We have read your terms in relation to exchange and introduction and regard them highly satisfactory. We herewith send you the number and description of the Latin Books used in the College last year........

The several *AHN-HENN Courses* are likewise being used with great success in **Rock Hill College, St. Joseph's College,** St. Joseph, Mo., and very many other Colleges, Academies and Schools of the Christian Brothers, and of the other Orders, all over the country.

At the same time they are also recommended, and used, by Professors of **Columbia, Yale, Williams,** and similar Colleges.

E. Steiger & Co., 25 Park Place, New York.

Attention is invited to the following:

The *AHN-HENN German, French,* and *Latin Courses* are published

in separate parts,

each one strongly bound and sold at a low price.

This division is **most important,** inasmuch as children who look with dread upon a large or bulky text-book. **cheerfully** enter upon the use of a **small volume** which, by being speedily completed, promises to **lighten their tasks** and **simplify their study.** — It is also a matter of much importance that a **large saving of expense** is at the same time effected by this division into parts.

For Educational Institutions the

Net Prices

of the **Text-books** published by ourselves (except *Keys* and *Wall-Charts*) are **25%** less than the Retail Prices quoted in our Lists. Forwarding Expenses extra.

For Introduction we furnish our Text-books with **50%** discount, and **for Exchange** we supply them either **free,** for copies in good condition, of the books actually displaced thereby, or else make the best possible terms, — according to circumstances. We invite correspondence in this respect.

The Vocabularies

attached to all the *AHN-HENN German, French,* and *Latin Text-books* and *Readers* are considered

most important and valuable.

They invariably give the pupil the **right** meaning of a word (which he would not always be certain to select from among the great number given in a Dictionary). They thus save a great amount of time and vexation both to pupil and teacher, while, at the same time, they do away with much unnecessary labor and ensure the **most satisfactory results.**

The Wall-Charts

German, French, Latin — are **unique,** and considered a great help in elementary instruction.

The several Keys

of the *AHN-HENN German, French,* and *Latin Text-books* and *Readers* will be furnished only upon the direct application of a Teacher to the Publishers.

E. Steiger & Co., 25 Park Place, **New York.**